Cadence and Rhyming and Feet

Kea Warren

Cadence and Rhyming and Feet © 2023
Kea Warren

All rights reserved.

No part of this publication may be reproduced, stored in a retrieval system, or transmitted, in any form or by any means, electronic, mechanical, photocopying, recording or otherwise, without the prior written permission of the presenters.

Kea Warren asserts the moral right to be identified as author of this work.

Presentation by *BookLeaf Publishing*

Web: www.bookleafpub.com

E-mail: info@bookleafpub.com

ISBN: 9789357441797

First edition 2023

To Sarah. Miss you, Bear.

ACKNOWLEDGEMENT

Thank you to my family, whose love and constant support has always been a guiding light through the hardest of times. Thank you to Arizona State University, specifically Mike Smith, Angela Huster, and Chris Morehart, for giving me the opportunities I needed to spread my wings. Thank you to Dr. Aaron Clay for helping me through the tough times. And finally, thank you to the pet owners who let me borrow their pets. You know who you are.

PREFACE

Google tells me that a preface is where you should explain why you are qualified to write something. I'm qualified to write poetry as I am a human with emotions and a decent grasp of the English language. Like everyone else, I've struggled and fallen. Somewhere along the line, though, someone handed me a pen and paper and I haven't stopped writing since.

Baking, Part 1

Baking is my favorite brand of science
Unwavering fundamentals stand ready,
The feeding of yeast,
The kneading of dough.
But that isn't all, you know.
Chemistry is a fickle mistress,
As some baking attempts have shown.
The wrong altitude or the wrong type of bowl
Can easily spell DOOM for your loaf.
Like most forms of applied chemistry,
Objectively,
A steady hand is required.

The Difference of a Day

How stark,
The whiplash suffered,
In the difference of a day.
On one, your helpful, joyful smile,
Your bright and cheery way.
The next was full of sorrow
Couldn't even beg you to stay.
How to find the silver lining,
No single soul can say,
But as time goes on without you,
We'll have to find a way.

I Know My Worth

I am a student
Of Curie and Franklin.
I'm am an heiress to Hedy Lamar.
Raised to test the limits,

Here to push the status quo,
An innovator
A scientist
A revolutionary in my own right

Uncompromising
Unwavering
Proud of where I've been
And proud of where I'm going

I've made my peace with circumstance
I never liked him anyway.
And like his brother, expectations,
I'm better off without.

Uplifting others
And even myself.
I've found joy in my own smile
And solace in my own laugh.

Moving forward,
Ever faster,
To an unknown future
Where self love I have mastered.

I smile at the goddess
Hiding in my mirror
I can finally see her joy
Her smile's never been clearer.

Baking, Part 2

5

Baking is my favorite kind of art.
The final product needs a pleasing taste,
That's a fact,
But there are four more sense that must be
delighted.
No matter how delicious it might be,
An ugly loaf won't sell.
So a baker needs to knead,
To temper sweet with salt.
And yet, while honoring all the rules and
requirements,
Chemistry can't prove the best of bread or cake.
Subjectively,
That's why I bake.

Hummingbird Song

Over the yucca,
Amid dusky skies and stars,
A hummingbird sings.

Saguaro

Towering cactus,
Arms raised to greet the morning,
Desert guardian

Dust Bowl

The sun beating down
A river flows no longer
The parched earth cries out

Thunderhead

9

The skies open up
Heaven Herself is weeping
A river reborn

Flash Flood

Raindrops fill the chasm
White water rapids from drought
The arid land drowns.

Stirred

Love is not just romance
Fair damsels and their knights
Love is when a heart is stirred
By empathy or kindness
Compassion or concern

Certainly,
a heartfelt note
or a warm embrace can show it
But the subtler acts of love go missed.

"Have you eaten today?"
Or "Let me know you're home safe"
If only such things were seen as they are
The stirring of one heart for another.

Hearts have a language of their own
That tongues can never speak
But if we learned to hear them
The world might be a kinder place.

Limericks are Hard

There once was a girl from Tempe
Taught singing and dancing at three
But only til four
Not one second more
For her evenings she always kept free.

A Tanka about Us

The nervous laughter
Posturing to impress you
A vibrant pink blush
Now sitting in silent bliss
No more nerves but still blushing.

The Dreadful Silence

Silence is peace to some
Meditative
Prescriptive
Therapeutic
Without interruption or distraction
Alone with their thoughts.

It is hell to others
Dead air festers
Worries
Anxiety
Woe
A cacophony of silence overwhelms the mind.

Worthy

15

Even when your heart is broken
Even when the road is rough
You are always worthy
You are always enough

Do not let the world damper
The loving soul you are inside
You are always worthy
Hold your head with pride.

Even when the world is burning
Have the strength to call their bluff
You are always worthy
You are always enough.

Naked; or a Poem Written in Plath's Keywords

Once upon a literature class,
We gutted "the Applicant" by Sylvia Plath.
It warped my brain,
It tested my limits,
And here is the fruit of my labor:

Naked
That word is guaranteed
to make someone uncomfortable
Somewhere, someone would be ashamed of me.

But my fearlessness is the key
It's a snare
It's a hook
I know it made you look

In ten, or twenty, or twenty-five years
Regardless of your age
Such word embody someone's fears
The fear of openness
Or a conversation killed by a slip of the tongue
From crutch to crotch
Beasts to breasts.

You! Where is your hand?
And you! Where do you stand?
How does censorship shape your life?

The last image
A conversation gives
Had best be
Shatterproof
Bulletproof
Waterproof
Lest it be lost to the ages.
A thousand messages given,
But only the most stark recalled.

And that is the life that I wish for myself
Being memorable
Only wanting
To make people take notice
To make them willing
And able to talk
Here
I
Am
Look at me
Notice me
Know me
Love me
Don't try to excuse my actions

Show no sorrow
Show no shame
Whatever I say is what I mean
This sort of thing
Is really
what's missing.

Open an eye
Or many
I don't care
Bring me bombs
like this to drop

Stop
Take stock of your life
Hone your blade
Sharpen your knife

In the face of discomfort, sweetie,
A person will start
Thumb their nose
then question their heart
Come out in the open
Or onto the roof
Stand proud
and give them the proof

Now is the time
and time is the ticket

It works on stiff collars
and men with crisp dollars

Is this wrong?
Tell me.
Is it right to change how we speak?
Do you believe it aloud
but then grit your teeth?

Teacups hit their saucers,
Rubber hits the road,
And salt meets the wound
When someone has to bite their lip
Hide their thoughts
Tighten their grip.
How much is lost to "polite conversation"?

Hide not in the closet
Nor anywhere, doll,
Find a place where you can stand tall.
Speak your truth and free your soul
Whomever is listening
Will forever carry a piece of you
In their heart
In their mind
In the depths of their soul.
Brace yourself
For the harsh words,
For some minds remain closed tight

Some sort of stitches
sew shut their eyes
No poultice nor herbs
No drugs
Serve as remedy

In the black of night
or silver of dawn
the false hope of day?
Where does it fit?
I mean, censoring this?

Will you dissolve into tears?
Crying from laughter
Or laughing from crying?
Living
Dying

Life's all too serious to be such a joke.
Broken glass
Melted gold
Truly, nothing to behold

Simmer in heaven
Or cook in hell
Marry me or bury me
Hate or love me

Just hear my words
This is my chance
Now is my time
To tell you all

The world is too incredible to be so damned
sensitive.

Bouncy Ball Brain

Inside my head
Instead of brains
I have a rubber ball
It bounces without a care
Off floor and roof and wall
Where it ends up going
No normal mind can tell
I might end up in sunny Spain
Or the seventh ring of hell
While this may sound funny
To those who do not know
The struggle stays the same
I wish the bounce would go.

An Overturned Stone

The shovel meets dirt
A clang startles the digger
A new piece is found

Santa Monica

The salty spray of the ocean
The chorus of seals and gulls
Their song entwined with the screams of delight
From children far above
Barkers raise their voices
Promising wonders not yet seen
Beside them amber kernels burst to life
next to the cotton candy machine
Amidst the sounds and songs
Suddenly, a FLASH
A startled looking face
A photographer saving
The bright and noisy place.

www.ingramcontent.com/pod-product-compliance
Lightning Source LLC
LaVergne TN
LVHW021339200726
843509LV00014B/2586